REI
CORNBREAD
· AND ·
YANKEE
COFFEE

REBEL CORNBREAD

·AND·

YANKEE

COFFEE

AUTHENTIC
CIVIL WAR COOKING

·AND·

CAMARADERIE

GARRY FISHER

CRANE HILL
PUBLISHERS

Every effort has been made to trace the copyright holders. Crane Hill Publishers apologizes for any unintentional omissions and would be pleased, in such cases, to add an acknowledgment in future editions.

Illustrated by Harry Blair

Published by Crane Hill Publishers
www.cranehill.com

Printed in the United States of America

Library of Congress Cataloging-in-Publication Data

Fisher, Garry D., 1956-
  Rebel cornbread and Yankee coffee : Civil War campfire cooking /
Garry D. Fisher.
  p. cm.
Includes bibliographical references and index.
ISBN 1-57587-175-0
  1. Cookery, American. 2. United States—History—Civil War,
1861-1865. I. Title.

  TX715 .F535 2001
  641.5973—dc21
  2001047007

10   9   8   7   6   5   4   3   2   1

In memory of my great-great grandfather,

Private Lacy Howard Lott,

Captain Max Van Den Corput's Battery,

"Cherokee" Light Artillery

C. S. A.

CONTENTS

PREFACE

I bought my first book about the War between the States when I was eight years old, and I have been fascinated with this era of American history ever since. Over time, however, I began reading less about the great battles and generals, and more about the common soldiers—those nameless, often faceless men, including my own ancestors, who so bravely endured the terror and deprivation of a war that claimed more than 600,000 American lives. In particular, I found myself drawn to the vivid memoirs of old men who, sensing life's approaching end, committed to paper the memories of a war they had fought as youths decades earlier—a war that was the defining event of their entire generation.

While their books and letters varied widely in content and viewpoint, I noticed two common themes: food and pastimes. The writers might have been hazy on certain events, and they might have scrambled a few facts about particular battles. But these old soldiers, whether they had worn Blue or Gray, could paint word pictures of army cooking so vivid that I sometimes found my mouth watering as if I, too, were sitting famished around the cook fire, impatiently awaiting my supper, playing a game of checkers. Other memories they painted of nearly starving, or of picking worms and maggots out of slop not fit for human consumption, had the power either to turn my stomach or move me to tears.

The recipes in *Rebel Cornbread and Yankee Coffee* document the typical diet of the rank-and-file soldiers in the field. Unlike many so-called Civil War recipes, those included here are not simply "inspired" by camp cooking; nor do they reflect the culinary experience of the more fortunate senior officers. Instead, I have attempted to record the real thing, culled directly from the memoirs and letters of common soldiers from both sides. I have worked to make them as authentic as possible so that the reader can, in some small way, share the experience with those men now long dead. Some recipes are actually pretty tasty. Others clearly bear the mark of desperation. I present them here just as our ancestors knew them, along with some of the songs and leisure activities that rounded out life for the common soldiers at the front. Enjoy.

FEEDING THE ARMIES

Feeding the pre–Civil War United States Army was a relatively simple matter. The army itself consisted of only about 16,000 men, most of whom were located in small, static garrisons scattered throughout the country and across the burgeoning frontier.

Providing the army with the necessary food and supplies was the responsibility of the Army Quartermaster Department, commanded by the Quartermaster General of the army. Within the Quartermaster Department was the Army Subsistence Department, overseen by the Commissary General. To this department fell the direct responsibility for feeding the army's soldiers.

During the years that followed the Mexican War of 1846–48, the Subsistence Department had developed an efficient supply system suited to the needs of peacetime. Under this system, which was overseen at the local level by brigade and regimental quartermasters and commissary officers, garrisons in or near cities and towns acquired the bulk of their foodstuffs from the local economies. Frontier garrisons and other remote posts were regularly resupplied by army supply trains run by the army or its contractors. The greatest struggle faced by these quartermasters was simply keeping up with the mountains of paperwork required by the peacetime army for each supply requisition.

The outbreak of the American Civil War in 1861 nearly strained the peacetime supply system to its breaking point. Both the Federal and Confederate governments suddenly found themselves confronting the near-Herculean task of feeding hundreds of thousands of men under arms. To make matters worse, the requirements of active campaigning meant that the armies,

During the years that followed the Mexican War of 1846–48, the Subsistence Department had developed an efficient supply system suited to the needs of peacetime.

instead of remaining in static positions, were on the move for months at a time. Just keeping up with them became a huge challenge. Both the Federal and Confederate Quartermaster Departments did their best to meet the needs of the men in the field. Even so, neither Billy Yank nor Johnny Reb could ever take having a full belly for granted.

The Confederate Supply System

The newly created Confederate States of America faced a tremendous task in even assembling an army, not to mention building the infrastructure to support it. From the beginning, feeding the tens of thousands of men who flocked to the defense of the South severely strained the resources of the new nation. After only a few months, the army began experiencing food shortages. The monumental logistical problems associated with feeding so many men under arms were further compounded by the large number of inexperienced officers and quartermasters in the new army. Many of these citizen-soldiers simply did not know the proper military procedures for how to draw and issue the rations that would keep their men fit and well fed.

Confederate President Jefferson Davis, a West Point graduate and former United States Secretary of War, appointed his lifelong friend and fellow West Pointer, Lucius Bellinger Northrop, to the post of Commissary General of the Confederacy in 1861. Northrop, who was a physician in Charleston, South Carolina, before the war, had little practical knowledge about running the subsistence bureau

Lucius Bellinger Northrop

of a large army. Obstinate, condescending, intolerant of the

suggestions of others, and obsessed with red tape, Northrop was an

extremely unpopular man accused of bungling and ineptitude by

scores of civilians and soldiers alike. In fact, the Confederate Senate

considered, but ultimately defeated, a motion in early 1864 to remove

him from office. Calls for his resignation continued, however, and he

was finally removed from office on February 15, 1865.

Despite his lack of popularity, Northrop's record shows that he actually performed his job more effectively than history has claimed, considering the disadvantages under which he and the poorly organized Army Subsistence Bureau struggled. The underfunded bureau had to deal with the devaluation of Confederate currency, the loss of vast food-producing areas of the Confederacy to federal occupation forces, and unscrupulous army contractors bent on making a profit at the soldiers' expense. The department also had to contend with a chronic lack of shipping containers such as barrels, kegs, and sacks, as well as corruption on the part of some lower-level commissary officials.

But of all the difficulties Northrop and his department faced, the greatest was the lack of available transportation. From the beginning, the system of railroads within the Confederacy was inadequate to meet the needs of a nation at war. Not a single mile of new track was laid in the South during the entire war; indeed, Confederate authorities found it nearly impossible just to maintain the existing rails and rolling stock. By the latter part of 1862, the whole system was beginning to deteriorate rapidly. While tons of valuable foodstuffs from rich agricultural areas like the Shenandoah

Valley in Virginia sat rotting on shipping docks around the country,

Confederate soldiers were forced to survive on half rations—all for

want of available transportation. Compounding these problems, the

Quartermaster Department and the
Subsistence Bureau often had great
difficulty in getting the available
supply stocks to the right place at
the right time. This was a particular
problem during periods of active

> **Aside from rations issued by the army, southern soldiers took advantage of donations and packages of food from the folks back home.**

campaigning, when unexpected changes in plans caused by the

fortunes of war could cause the army to go in one direction while the

supplies it needed went in another.

Aside from rations issued by the army, southern soldiers took

advantage of donations and packages of food from the folks back

home. Officials from soldier relief organizations, soldiers returning

from furlough or convalescence, visiting relatives, and family slaves

dispatched from home would bring with them gifts of food

whenever possible. A large number of packages also arrived by train, especially during the first two years of the war when Confederate rail transportation was still functional. Although delayed trains would occasionally cause the contents of the packages to spoil before they reached the eager hands of the hungry men at the front, these homemade care packages, filled with meat, fruit, pies, and other delicacies, had an electric effect on morale.

> Sometimes, farmers would come into the camps to peddle their goods; at other times the soldiers would seek them out.

Sutlers, civilian merchants who followed in the paths of the armies, also provided an unofficial source of food and other supplies—assuming the soldiers were able to pay the sutler's often-exorbitant prices. In general, sutlers were less common in the South than they were in the North. As the war ground on, their negative image and the increasing shortages of wares made sutlers less important as an alternative supply source, although they trailed the southern armies right up until the end.

More often than not, soldiers found it easier to cut out the middleman and buy directly from the farmers themselves. Sometimes, farmers would come into the camps to peddle their goods; at other times the soldiers would seek them out. Soldiers short on money often resorted to barter. In fact, as the war continued and the value of Confederate currency continued to deteriorate, most farmers refused to accept cash payments, making barter the rule rather than the exception.

Despite such informal trading, the necessity of feeding large numbers of men in the field often required the Confederate armies to forage for food by sending organized details of soldiers to local farms to requisition critical food supplies. In return, the army issued the farmers official receipts that, in theory, they could present to the local quartermaster for cash reimbursement. However, the eventual worthlessness of Confederate currency meant that many farmers were simply out whatever they "donated" to the army.

Because they fought the war almost exclusively on southern soil, the Confederate armies did try to go through the motions of paying the local populace for the foodstuffs they requisitioned, and of maintaining discipline among the troops doing the foraging. Nevertheless, despite official orders that strictly prohibited theft of civilian food and supplies, unauthorized "foraging" became a significant problem as the war continued, and as the quality and quantity of army supplies dwindled. Incidents of theft were worst in areas abandoned by the civilian population because of approaching Yankee troops or an impending battle. William A. Fletcher, a private in Hood's Texas Brigade, writing of the results of a particularly successful raid on a local farm, wryly noted that " 'Foraging' was the word applied for such outings during the war—in civil life it is called 'shoplifting'." Bell Wiley, in his book *The Life of Johnny Reb,* quotes another Confederate soldier, Robert M. Gill, who, in a June 1862 letter to his wife, stated: "I now have some idea of the devastating effects of an army marching through the Country. Our soldiers act outrageously, not withstanding the strict orders and their sure execution in reference to the destruction of private property. Our soldiers have not left a fat hog, chicken, turkey, goose, duck, or eggs or onions behind."

Montgomery Cunningham Meigs

The Federal Supply System

Despite the tremendous advantage of having inherited an existing military infrastructure, reliable railroads, and the financial wherewithal of the United States government, the Federal army's supply efforts also got off to a rocky start. The nearly overnight expansion of the army from sixteen thousand professional soldiers to a force of more than a hundred thousand inexperienced soldier-civilians placed a huge burden upon the army's existing supply systems. Overseeing this tremendous effort was Brigadier General (later Major General) Montgomery Cunningham Meigs, appointed

Much of the blame for the early food shortages lay with inexperienced federal officers and quartermasters.

to the position of Quartermaster General of the army on May 14, 1861, after the previous holder of the position, Joseph E. Johnson, resigned to fight for the Confederacy. (In 1864, Meigs would become known for proposing that two hundred acres of Confederate General Robert E. Lee's property at Arlington, Virginia, be used for burying United States soldiers. And so began Arlington National Cemetery.) Throughout the four years of the war, Meigs, the Quartermaster Department, and the Army Subsistence Department under Colonel (later Brigadier General) Joseph P. Taylor struggled against scheming military contractors and the sheer magnitude of the task of providing food and equipment to the largest army yet to operate on American soil.

Despite these efforts, the Federal army fell victim to the same sorts of temporary food shortages that plagued their Confederate opponents. In the East, the Army of the Potomac experienced occasional food shortages as late as the fall of 1863. Like the Confederacy's western armies, the Federal army's western forces also fared relatively worse than their eastern comrades, experiencing occasional food shortages right up to the end of the war.

Much of the blame for the early food shortages lay with inexperienced Federal officers and quartermasters who, like their Confederate counterparts, had to learn the hard way how to requisition and distribute rations to their hungry troops. Also, the Federal quartermaster and commissary departments were no more successful than their counterparts in the Confederacy at ensuring that the supply trains caught up with the army during the confusion of active campaigning.

Out-and-out corruption appears to have been exaggerated by the soldiers of the day on both sides. Lax procedures, the prerogatives of rank, and just plain laziness also conspired to rob those at the bottom of the distribution network—the men doing the fighting and dying—of much of their daily ration. This was especially true with regard to critical foods such as vegetables. In one example of the challenge faced by both sides, federal General William Rosecrans, commander of the Army of the Cumberland, launched an investigation into the cause of an outbreak of scurvy during the winter of 1862. The investigation discovered that his soldiers had not received more than three issues of vegetables during an entire twelve-month period, even though records showed that a hundred barrels of vegetables per day had been issued. Instead, staff officers, their families, and the various corps, divisional, and brigade commissaries had almost completely claimed the entire distribution, leaving the regimental commissaries, which supplied the needs of the rank and file, with virtually no vegetable allotments whatsoever.

Like his Rebel counterparts, however, Billy Yank didn't rely solely upon the army to supply all that was needed to keep body and soul together. Northern soldiers, too, were the grateful recipients of packages sent by rail from the folks back home. While these packages may not have always been as important for providing the essentials as were those received by their Rebel counterparts, it's fair to say that their impact on Yankee morale was just as significant.

Sutlers also plied their trade among Yankee encampments, selling pies, cakes, fruit, candy, and other delicacies to those who could afford the high markup. And, just as they did when the southern army was nearby, a few enterprising local civilians entered the camps, intent on selling whatever they had available to any Yankee eager to add

> **Like his Rebel counterparts, Billy Yank didn't rely solely upon the army to supply all that was needed to keep body and soul together.**

a little variety to his diet. Also, some Northerners, intent on escaping the monotony of the standard army diet, dined in the homes of willing southern civilians, either as guests or as paying customers.

Like the Confederate army, the Federal army also relied on foraging from southern civilians to augment army rations. Foraging was usually conducted by specially formed groups of enlisted men under the command of a lieutenant or captain. Acting on the authority of a high-ranking officer, these foraging parties scoured the southern countryside in search of edibles. If the donor claimed loyalty to the Union, the commander of the foraging detail would issue him a receipt for all requisitioned foodstuffs and supplies. The burdens of collecting payment and proving Union loyalty were left to the unhappy host.

Surviving records show that the army's senior- and mid-level commanders generally made genuine efforts to enforce the army's orders governing the conduct of foraging parties and issued strict directives designed to protect southern civilians from acts of plundering. Unfortunately, the efforts of the junior officers charged with enforcing these directives were uneven. The enlisted men in their commands were their friends, neighbors, and relatives; many of these lieutenants and captains were in no hurry to discipline trusted comrades found stealing from a people they viewed as the enemy. As a result, many Yankee soldiers simply took whatever they wished whenever they wanted it, believing that the Southerners had earned their misery as traitors to the Union.

Finally, and mostly confined to the Yankee army, was the concept of the company fund. The theory behind the fund was simple: Any company commander could sell back to the commissary any extra food supplies. The cash generated by the sale would then go into a company fund for purchase of supplemental food items not available through the commissary. The company commander or his designate administered the fund. However, what sounded good in theory seldom worked out in practice. Many officers, themselves neophyte soldiers, knew nothing about such a fund. Others considered administering such funds too much work and simply avoided them. Finally, a few dishonest types even appropriated the funds for their own use.

RATIONS, COOKING ARRANGEMENTS, AND EQUIPMENT

Unlike the soldiers of the Civil War, the modern American soldier eats a diet scientifically designed to be nutritious and—if not the most varied and appetizing—at least safe and palatable. In the field, he (or she) is amply supplied with T-Rations (Tray Rations) and MREs (Meals—Ready to Eat). Back on base, mess halls serve virtually unlimited quantities of food prepared by trained cooks. And soldiers stationed stateside who wish to cook for themselves can find a supermarket-sized selection of meat, produce, and sundries at the post commissary.

Civil War soldiers, on the other hand, survived on a diet that was nutritionally incomplete and maddeningly monotonous, at best. At worst, it could cause severe illness—or even death—due to spoilage, insect infestation, and general ignorance about basic hygiene. That men forced to eat such fare could survive is itself a tribute to their courage and determination.

Throughout the war, both sides experimented with the contents, quality, and size of the rations supplied to soldiers. Despite struggling against occasional food shortages at the front caused by complex wartime logistics, the United States, with its mighty industrial establishment and abundant financial resources, was in a much better position than the Confederacy to supply the needs of its soldiers. Consequently, the North focused its efforts on adding variety to the standard army diet and making it more abundant and nutritious. The South, on the other hand, with its limited industrial capability, disintegrating railroads, and dependence on cotton exports to finance the war, slowly strangled as the United States Navy blockaded its ports. As the war progressed, large tracts of fertile farmland were lost to the advancing northern armies. As a result, the Confederacy struggled throughout the war to find suitable substitutes for items in the standard army ration that were in short supply or no longer available, and to find ways to reduce the cost and size of the army's rations without starving its soldiers.

The Federal Army Ration

When war broke out in the spring of 1861, the standard daily ration of the United States Army had changed little since 1775. The most noteworthy modification occurred in 1832 when President

Andrew Jackson, bowing to pressure from the temperance movement sweeping the nation, ordered that coffee and sugar be substituted for the soldiers' daily liquor ration. With that exception, the men who fought between 1861 and 1865 ate a ration their grandfathers and great-grandfathers might have consumed during the American Revolution.

According to the Revised U. S. Army Regulations, July 1861, the official daily ration consisted of the following:

> *20 ounces of fresh or salt beef, or 12 ounces of either pork or bacon; 18 ounces of flour or soft bread, or 12 ounces of hard bread or 20 ounces of corn meal; 1.2 ounces of beans or 1.6 ounces of rice or either 3 ounces of desiccated potatoes or 2 ounces of desiccated mixed vegetables; 1.6 ounces of green coffee or 1.28 ounces of tea; 0.32 gills of vinegar, 2.4 ounces of sugar and 0.6 ounces of salt.*

Compared to the allotments of other armies, this was a generous quantity. For example, the British army's standard ration was about one-fifth smaller, while the average French soldier ate only about half as much. Despite its relative largesse, the U.S. War Department authorized an increase on August 3, 1861, that significantly added to the amount of hard bread, beans, potatoes, and roasted coffee per ration. By June of 1864, however, the army concluded that the increase had led to an unnecessary waste of food and revoked the increase, except for the provision allowing quartermasters to substitute fresh or processed vegetables for other parts of the ration.

The United States Army, like other established armies around the world, constantly experimented with new and improved ways to provide nutrition for its soldiers. In 1857, the army introduced what it called "desiccated vegetables," a vegetable concentrate reported by many Civil War soldiers to be about as tasty as chopped straw. Often referred to as "desecrated vegetables" or "baled hay" by the men in the ranks, desiccated

> **The army constantly experimented with new and improved ways to provide nutrition for its soldiers.**

vegetables were large, dry cakes about two inches thick, composed of compressed, finely chopped cabbage, carrots, turnips, onions, beets, and string beans. Heavily peppered to reduce spoilage, the cakes expanded dramatically in size when soaked in water, which made them good for little else than a soup ingredient.

During periods when the army expected to be actively campaigning beyond the range of its supply trains, the soldiers ate what was referred to as the marching ration: three days' worth of hardtack, salt pork, coffee, salt, and sugar. Even the greenest recruit quickly learned that the marching ration had significance beyond just its contents: When the order came to draw three days' rations, it meant the enemy was near, and the likelihood of "seeing the elephant," as the old veterans referred to combat, a near certainty.

The Confederate Army Ration

Confederate military authorities originally adopted the pre–August 1861 United States Army ration as the standard for the newly formed Confederate States Army. Almost from the beginning, however, this proved optimistic. Food shortages occurred as early as July 1861 in some areas, and Confederate authorities were forced to reduce the standard ration less than a year later in April 1862. However, further cuts were soon necessary. In January 1863, the Confederate government reduced the daily quantity of salted meat issued to soldiers in the Army of Northern Virginia to a mere one-quarter pound per man. This lasted until the fall of 1864, when it was increased to one third of a pound. At the same time as he increased the meat ration, however, the commissary general was forced to reduce the Army of Northern Virginia's flour or cornmeal ration to one pound from its previous level of one pound, four ounces. Rations were also further reduced in the western armies: In August 1863, the commissary general reduced the meat ration of the Army of Mississippi to one third of a pound, where it remained as the defacto standard for the rest of the war in all the western armies of the Confederacy.

Confederate soldiers were also familiar with the marching ration. However, continual food shortages meant that Johnny Reb's marching ration often consisted of cornbread, bacon, and water in lieu of the officially prescribed ration. Also, the term "three days' rations" tended to be optimistic: The reduced quantities of the normal ration meant that the average Rebel found it far easier to simply eat his entire marching ration all in one sitting, rather than go through the hassle of carrying it while in action.

Cooking Arrangements

Early in the war, both sides attempted to establish the institution of the company cook. The Federals, in particular, continued throughout the war to try to cook food in large quantities by detailing two men per company specifically for that purpose. Excused from both drill and combat, men detailed as cooks generally were older or suffered from chronic health trouble or other problems. Rarely were they chosen for their particular culinary expertise. Captain John G. B. Adams, writing in his book *Reminiscences of the 19th Massachusetts Regiment,* summed up the prevailing opinion of Federal army cooks:

> *A company cook is a peculiar being: he generally knows less about cooking than any other man in the company. Not being able to learn the drill, and too dirty to appear on inspection, he is sent to the cook house to get him out of the ranks.*

Preparation of food *en masse* never really caught on in the Confederate army, mostly due to the lack of available cooking equipment and the independent nature of the Confederate soldier.

Early on, the army tried its best to set up bakeries at the brigade level, but the hardships of active campaigning soon forced it to abandon this system. Records show, however, that food was centrally prepared and delivered to the men in the trenches during the sieges of both Vicksburg and Petersburg.

By and large, the "mess" system or individual cooking prevailed on both sides, especially during active campaigning. A mess consisted of four to ten men, usually friends or relatives, who elected to share cooking responsibilities. A man who could cook was held in high esteem by his less-talented comrades. He could often bargain his way out of other unpleasant duties in return for cooking for his mess. "As I was a good cook," noted William A. Fletcher in his memoir *Rebel Private: Front and Rear,* "the boys were always ready to fill my mess duties if I would cook." Occasionally, men on both sides would employ the services of a black servant to do the cooking and cleanup. This apparently became less and less common as the war ground on, especially in the southern army, which had difficulty even feeding its fighting men, let alone a large number of body servants and slaves.

Utensils and Equipment

When they managed to get some food, the next big problem confronting the men in both armies was how to cook it. In the early days, before either side had learned the hard practicalities of war, the green volunteer regiments would arrive in their training camps with heavy cook chests, one per mess. Loaded with every imaginable cooking implement, the chests were so heavy they had to be drawn in wagons. Carlton McCarthy, a member of the famous Richmond Howitzers, looked back with amusement at these elaborate chests in his excellent memoir *Detailed Minutiae of Soldier Life in the Army of Northern Virginia:*

> *In addition to each man's private luggage, each mess, generally of from five to ten men, drawn together by similar tastes and associations, had its outfit, consisting of a large camp chest containing skillet, frying pan, coffee boiler, bucket for lard, coffee box, salt box, meal box, flour box, knives, forks, spoons, plates, cups, etc., etc. These chests were so large that two strong men had all they could do to get one of them into the wagon.*

When in camp, Federal company cooks generally preferred boiling food to frying or broiling it, since boiling was the easiest and fastest way to prepare large quantities of food. To do this, they used an assortment of mess kettles and mess pans. Mess kettles were large sheet-iron cylinders that measured anywhere from thirteen to fifteen inches high and seven to twelve inches in diameter. A mess pan, by comparison, was a six-quart metal bowl, measuring about twelve inches in diameter at the top.

mess pan

Just as it suffered from food and other shortages, the Confederate army also lacked an adequate supply of cooking equipment and eating utensils. The shortage became so dire that Colonel Robert V. Richardson, commanding the Twelfth Tennessee Cavalry Regiment, was moved to submit the following plea to his brigade commander in October 1863:

> *I have not a single vessel to cook one morsel of*
> *bread. My cooking has to be done as we can beg the*

*citizens to do it. This practice is exceedingly
deleterious. It leads to straggling and
demoralization. For God and the country's sake,
make your fair-promising but never-complying
quartermaster send me skillets, ovens, pots or
anything that will bake bread or fry meat.... Send
me skillets 225 in number. I cannot fight any more
until I get something to cook in.*

Many Rebels improvised by crafting their own implements.
"The boys have made frying pans out of plates and picked up
vessels until they ask [General Braxton] Bragg no odds," remarked
J. H. Puckett, a Texas private in the Confederate Army of
Tennessee, in an October 1863 letter to his wife. A captured metal
canteen could be split in half by exploding a little gunpowder inside

mess kettle

it, and the halves fashioned into skillets and plates. Likewise, a stick, its forks whittled to sharp points, made a passable fork or a spit upon which to roast bacon or beef.

Still, shortages of cooking equipment among the southern armies were widespread. It was a lucky company (anywhere from fifty to one hundred men) that had more than two or three frying pans at one time. So highly valued were they that the men, rather than risk losing a skillet from a company wagon while on the march, assigned it to a trustworthy individual, who marched

with the panhandle slipped down the barrel of his rifle.

Although much better supplied with cooking and eating equipment than their opponents, Federal troops also had to contend with shortages. True to their entrepreneurial heritage, the Yankee soldiers often solved their predicament by forming a business venture known as a "stock company." Each "stockholder"

"spider"

contributed an equal amount of money toward the purchase of a "spider," a three-legged, cast-iron skillet, from one of the ever-present camp sutlers. Responsibility for carrying the skillet on the march rotated among the stockholders, with the understanding that the man carrying it that day got to use it first that night.

Enterprising stock companies often rented out their assets, making a tidy profit for their owners. In his book, *Three Years in the*

Army, Charles E. Davis, the historian of the Thirteenth Massachusetts, relates a humorous anecdote about the respect such men of means were accorded by their comrades:

> *... a stockholder in the "Joint Stock Frying Pan Company" was looked upon as a man of consequence. Being treated with kindness and civility by his comrades, life assumed a roseate hue to the shareholders in this great company, in spite of their deprivations. It was flattering to hear one's self mentioned in terms of praise by some impecunious comrade who wished to occupy one side of it while you were cooking.*

EDIBLES
AND
INDIGESTIBLES

Together with his messmates, the soldier learned to experiment and improvise with the limited ingredients available to add variety to meals, and to limit the dangers of eating food that was often spoiled or contaminated. The commissary systems of the two armies tried their best to provide a sufficient variety of nutritious food. However, food science itself was in its infancy: Despite some improvements over the years before the war, the basic army diet was still loaded with saturated fat, and low in fiber, vitamins, and minerals.

This chapter describes how the common soldiers prepared the food they ate daily in the field. A few of these concoctions were unique to one side or the other. Most, however, were well known by both Yankees and Rebels.

Hardtack

Army bread. Sheet-iron crackers. Hard bread. Worm castles. Whatever names a man called it, and no matter how much he despised it, hardtack was the heart of the army diet. This was especially true for Federal soldiers, who typically received nine to twelve squares of hardtack per day. Confederate soldiers, on the

other hand, ate more and more cornbread as the war ground on and

available foodstuffs were substituted for the official ration. Still,

owing to the capture of Federal supplies and the common practice

of rummaging through the haversacks of dead Yankees, Johnny Reb

was well acquainted with the culinary delights of hardtack.

Hardtack was nothing more than an unleavened, three-

inch-square, flour and water

biscuit, usually about a

half-inch thick. Baked by

government contractors, its size

and toughness made it capable of

surviving for days in a haversack without crumbling into powder.

Despite soldiers' disparaging comments, hardtack was reasonably

nutritious and good tasting—when it was fresh. Therein lay the

problem: Unlike the airtight containers available today for shipping

and storing food, the containers used to store hardtack were simple

wooden boxes that allowed in water, air, and insects. The poor

quality of the storage containers was further underscored by transportation and distribution delays. Fifty-pound boxes of hardtack sometimes spent weeks or even months sitting on docks before reaching army supply trains. All too often, hungry soldiers would pry the lid off a long-awaited shipment of hardtack and find it moldy, wormy, full of weevils, or so hard a man had to soak it in water just to keep from breaking a tooth on it.

Because hardtack was not prepared by the soldiers themselves, the recipe at right differs from most others in *Rebel Cornbread and Yankee Coffee,* in that it was written for use in a modern kitchen, instead of in the field.

Many soldiers roasted their hardtack by holding it over a fire on a forked stick. Not only did roasting the hardtack add a little variety to an otherwise monotonous meal, it had the added benefit of ridding the cracker of any weevils in residence. Some men even embellished their roasted hardtack by topping it with butter, if available, or a portion of their sugar ration.

If a piece of hardtack fell off the roasting implement into the fire, it was promptly fished out, blown free of ashes, and stored for later use in the belief that burned hardtack helped relieve diarrhea.

Hardtack

4 cups presifted flour
2 teaspoons shortening
1 cup of water

In a large mixing bowl, combine the flour with the shortening. Mix them together with your hands until thoroughly blended. Add the water, and knead the mixture into dough, which should be stiff and elastic, and not at all sticky to the touch.

Place the dough on a counter or breadboard that has been dusted with flour. Using a heavy mallet, pound the dough out until it's about $1/2$-inch thick. (I use a rubber-headed shop mallet with a plastic bag or two on the head to prevent "skid marks" in the dough. Wooden mallets are good, too.) Next, fold the dough into 5 or 6 layers, and pound it out again. Repeat the pounding and folding process a total of 5 or 6 times.

Using a flour-dusted rolling pin, roll out the dough until it is smooth and about $1/4$-inch thick. Cut into 3-inch squares and place the squares on an ungreased cookie sheet. For added realism and better baking results, use a shish kebab skewer to poke 4 rows of 4 holes in each square.

Place the cookie sheet in a preheated oven and bake for about 35 minutes at 325°. After baking, turn off the heat and leave the hardtack in the oven until the oven is cool, in order to further dry it. The hardtack is now ready to eat. Makes 10–12 squares.

Confederate Skillet Cornbread

As previously mentioned, Confederate soldiers generally were issued either cornbread or cornmeal instead of hardtack or wheat flour. Because cornbread was the most common item in the daily ration, Johnny Reb grew as tired of cornbread as his Federal counterpart did of hardtack. Adrian Carruth, a soldier from Louisiana, summed up the general feeling about cornbread: "If any person offers me cornbread after this war comes to a close, I shall probably tell him to go to hell!"

The cornmeal used was often poor in quality—coarse and unsifted. But it was filling and often the only thing between a man's stomach and going hungry.

Confederate Skillet Cornbread

¹/₂ cup raw cornmeal
Bacon grease
Water
Salt

Put about a quarter of a day's ration (about ¹/₂ cup) of raw cornmeal into a bowl. Add a heaping spoonful of bacon grease, and work it into the meal until all the meal is dampened. Then slowly stir in water until the consistency is a cross between scrambled eggs and cold pudding. Salt to taste.

Coat the bottom of a small skillet with bacon grease. Heat over hot coals until the grease just starts to smoke. Now, pour the "dough" into the skillet. Make sure the cake of cornbread is slightly smaller than the bottom of the skillet; this will allow it to be turned over more easily. Smooth out the top with a spoon or fork. When the bottom is thoroughly browned, gently flip the cornbread over and cook until the other side is brown. Remove from the skillet and eat.

Often, not even cornbread was available. Instead, raw cornmeal was issued to the troops, one pound four ounces per man being the official daily ration. The soldiers made do by cooking their own sort of skillet cornbread from the ingredients at hand.

Salt Pork

Along with hardtack and cornbread, salt pork (or "sow belly," as the men on both sides often called it) represented the other major staple of the Civil War soldier's diet. Federal army rations included twelve ounces of salt pork per day, while Confederate soldiers made do with perhaps half that amount, at best.

Salt pork was simply pork skin, cut to include the underlying fat and a small amount of meat; the cut was then cured with salt to preserve it. As with hardtack, it was prepared to government specifications by a government contractor and shipped to army supply depots.

Raw salt pork, available in most supermarkets in the meat section (near the bacon) can be prepared in a number of ways.

Soldiers during the War between the States most commonly ate it fried, boiled, or broiled. (Bacon can be substituted for salt pork in these recipes, but for authenticity use the most thickly cut, fatty bacon you can find, such as chips and ends usually available by the boxful in the supermarket.)

Fried Salt Pork

The soldier's favorite, as it allowed him to collect the leftover grease for frying and baking.

¹/₄ lb. salt pork

Slice a ¹/₄-pound slab of salt pork into 3 equal parts.
Fry it in a pan until the fat is crisp and the meat thoroughly cooked.
Eat directly out of the pan or atop a square of hardtack.

In the Federal army, salt pork was frequently the only meat available to troops on the march. While the commissary sometimes distributed fresh meat when the army was in fixed encampments between campaigns, salt pork was still ubiquitous. Occasionally, bacon was issued in place of salt pork. However, the soldiers generally preferred salt pork, especially when actively campaigning: Not only did the salt in it keep it from going rancid quickly, but also, unlike bacon, a man could carry raw salt pork in his haversack without its fat draining off and staining his clothing, bedroll, and everything else in the surrounding three counties.

Even though salt pork was better suited to the soldiers' needs, surviving records and memoirs suggest that Confederate soldiers ate more bacon than salt pork. The reason was simply that the Confederate armies, chronically short of foodstuffs, relied heavily on supplies from the farms in their areas of operations. Since bacon, unlike salt pork, was a common item on most farms, the

Broiled Salt Pork

Often used when a skillet or other cooking implement was unavailable, broiling was less popular than frying because the grease could not be captured.

¹/₄-lb. slab of salt pork

Cut salt pork into 2 or 3 equal pieces and skewer them with a (nonpoisonous) stick or the ramrod of a rifle. Broil over an open fire until cooked through.

Eat it off the stick, or on a square of hardtack.

Boiled Salt Pork

Most commonly used when cooking was done centrally for the entire company.

1 large slab of salt pork
Water

Put a slab of salt pork large enough for an entire mess into a mess kettle. Add enough water to cover the salt pork by an inch or so, and boil it over a fire until thoroughly cooked. Drain the water and slice the salt pork into individual servings.

Serve on a square of hardtack.

defenders of the South ended up eating bacon or even ham. Nevertheless, frequent captures of Yankee supplies ensured that they had more than a passing familiarity with salt pork.

Sometimes, the scarcity of firewood or the proximity of enemy forces forced the men to eat raw salt pork. In such instances, a soldier would simply make do by putting the raw meat between squares of hardtack, sandwich style. (Obviously, eating raw salt pork is not something you should try, unless you really want to experience some of the rampant gastrointestinal illness that plagued both armies.)

In addition to being eaten alone or with hardtack, salt pork was a frequent ingredient in stews and soups. The soldiers also used its grease for frying other foods or to add as an ingredient to bread and flapjacks.

Coffee

Without a doubt, the most prized part of any Civil War soldier's ration was his coffee. Billy Yank, unlike his Confederate counterpart, enjoyed a comparatively ample supply of it: The daily Federal army ration was large enough for a man to make three or four pints of strong brew. Strangely enough, the coffee issued to the Federal boys was also the only part of their daily ration that was of a consistently high quality: The army's procurement officers ensured this by purchasing whole-bean coffee instead of ground coffee, which stood the risk of being mixed with sawdust or any manner of things by unscrupulous suppliers.

John Billings, a Federal army veteran, in his classic book *Hard Tack and Coffee,* wrote that coffee was consumed before meals, during meals, and after meals. Men drank it prior to going on guard duty, he noted, and then again after coming off duty. Even on the march, Billings observed, tired soldiers would often fall out of the column, boil up some coffee, take a nap, and then run like the dickens to overtake their companies before evening roll call. The

older veterans went so far as to grind their coffee, mix it with their sugar ration, and store the mixture in a small cloth bag to cut down the time required to make their beloved beverage. It wasn't for nothing that artillerymen and cavalrymen referred to the infantry as "coffee boilers."

The longer a man served, the stronger he tended to like his coffee. Since sugar oftentimes wasn't available, many soldiers came to prefer their coffee black. Another Federal veteran, F. Y. Hedley, in his book

Marching Through Georgia, summed up army coffee as "black as the face of a plantation, 'strong enough to float an iron wedge', and innocent of lacteal adulteration, it gave strength to the weary and heavy laden, and courage to the despondent and sick at heart."

In the Confederate army, coffee was in short supply from the beginning of the war. In fact, supplies became so lean that by January 1862 it began disappearing altogether from army rations. Americans on both sides of the Mason-Dixon have always loved their coffee, so the average Confederate soldier took that loss particularly hard. A. N. Erskine, a soldier in Hood's Texas Brigade, probably spoke for the entire Confederate army when he lamented in a letter to his wife, "How much I miss the good coffee I used to get at home. I would cheerfully pay a dollar for as much like it as I could drink."

Johnny Reb considered it a real treat to get his hands on some captured Yankee coffee. When he couldn't do that, he, like the folks back home, devised various coffee substitutes, such as sassafras tea and "coffee" made by boiling such things as chicory, potatoes, parched peanuts, peas, corn, or rye.

As a rule, soldiers preferred preparing their own coffee to drinking coffee brewed by the gallon by the company cook. A typical soldier prepared his coffee as follows.

Army Coffee
Green coffee beans
Water
Clean straining cloth
Sugar and milk as desired

If you really want to be authentic, and have gotten hold of some green (unroasted) coffee, you first will need to roast it—army cooking manuals called it "parching." Fill a skillet halfway with coffee beans and place it over a bed of glowing coals. Stir the beans frequently, making sure you stir from the bottom of the skillet so that the beans on the bottom rotate to the top. When the beans are about halfway browned, add a little water (about an ounce per pound of coffee). Keep stirring until the beans turn a deep brown, taking care to remove any that get scorched. Take the skillet off the fire and set it aside to cool. If you are using a cast-iron skillet, it will retain a lot of heat, so you may need to continue stirring the beans for a while to keep them from burning.

After the beans have cooled, you're ready to brew some coffee. Use a handful of cooled, roasted beans per cup of water. If you don't have access to a small hand grinder, you can grind the beans by piling them in a

(continued)

Army Coffee (continued)

mess tin and smashing them with the butt of a rifle or a rock.

Using either a 1-pint tin cup or an empty tin can rigged with a bailing wire handle, combine the pulverized beans with water. With a stick or a piece of fence rail as a holder, hang your "coffeepot" over the fire and boil the contents to the desired strength. The longer the coffee boils, the stronger the brew.

Remove the coffee from the fire and carefully strain it through a piece of cloth, such as clean flannel, into a drinking cup. Add sugar and milk if desired and drink. As an alternative, crumble a square of hardtack into a cup of freshly boiled coffee and eat the resulting mixture with a spoon. This was a favorite of Yankee soldiers on campaign.

Beef

Unlike his Yankee counterpart, Johnny Reb (when he had much to eat at all) ate a lot of beef. Along with cornmeal, beef served as the backbone of the Confederate army's daily ration. Sometimes, the men got their beef fresh off the hoof from herds of cattle driven along with the army. Other times, however, the rapid movements of active campaigning required that the cattle be slaughtered elsewhere and the meat shipped great distances for distribution to the soldiers.

Broiled Beef

This was the most common way of cooking fresh beef in either army.

1 sturdy stick, 3 feet long
1 8- to 10-oz. cut beef chuck
Seasoning as desired

Find a sturdy stick, about 3 feet long (make sure it's from a nonpoisonous plant). Using a knife, strip away about a foot or so of bark on one end. Thread 8–10 ounces of beef chuck onto the stick, taking advantage of any small natural "forks" in the stick to keep the meat from flopping around loosely. (If necessary, cut the meat into two smaller pieces.) Season if desired, and roast the meat to your taste over an open fire, turning it every few minutes to cook it evenly.

Fried Beef

Salt pork or bacon grease
1 8- to 10-oz. cut of beef chuck
Salt
Carrot or onion if desired

Put a small amount of grease from frying salt pork or bacon in the bottom of a cold frying pan. Heat the grease. Sprinkle the beef chuck with a pinch or two of salt. Place the meat in the heated pan and fry until cooked to your taste. Eat it right out of the pan with a square or two of hardtack. For variation, fry the meat with a sliced carrot and fresh onion.

With no refrigeration, the beef distributed to the soldiers was often spoiled and loaded with maggots. Confederate beef rations were generally of such poor quality that the soldiers took to referring to the beef as "mule." One Georgian, William R. Stillwell, summed up the prevailing view of beef, saying that the men "take it as it comes hare [sic] skin and dust and it is so rank that it can hardly be eat [sic]."

Despite its reliance on salt pork as the primary meat supply, the Federal army also slaughtered herds of cattle for fresh beef.

Beef Stew

1 8- to 10-oz. cut of beef chuck
Water
2 carrots per person, 1 potato per person,
and 1 onion per person
3 cups of army (white) beans
Salt
Flour

Cut the beef chuck into small cubes or strips to feed an entire mess (4–10 men). Place the beef in a mess kettle and add enough water to cover the meat by about an inch of water. Place the kettle over the fire and boil the meat until tender.

While the meat boils, wash and slice carrots, potatoes, and onions.

After the meat has boiled for about 45 minutes, add the vegetables and beans. Salt to taste and boil until the vegetables and beans are tender.

If desired, slowly stir in a little flour just before serving, and cook briefly to thicken the broth.

Occasionally, they received shipments of salted beef, or "salt horse," as the soldiers referred to it. Impregnated with enough salt to preserve it for at least two years, "salt horse" was not popular among the troops. Not only did it have to be soaked in water overnight to leach out enough salt to make the meat edible (which, coincidentally, also leached out the vitamins and minerals), but once cooked, the oftentimes ancient beef stank enough to grow hair on a cannonball. Sometimes, when issued unusually bad beef, the men would place the guilty piece of meat atop an empty hardtack box and carry it throughout the camp in a mock funeral procession—preferably in sight of the regiment's commander. After an appropriate eulogy, they then gave it a decent burial.

Men of both armies normally broiled their beef rations over an open fire, using either a stick or the ramrod of a rifle to skewer it. Occasionally, they also fried the meat either alone in a pan or with vegetables, when available. Beef was also boiled in soups and stews.

You'd be hard-pressed to find beef of as poor a grade as the

average Yankee or Confederate soldier put up with. However, an
inexpensive cut of beef chuck may at least give you an idea of
what they typically ate.

Skillygalee and Hell-Fired Stew

Federal troops invented skillygalee and hell-fired stew to vary
the blandness of the standard army ration and to dispose of old

Skillygalee
1 square of hardtack
Water
Salt pork grease
Salt

Place a single square of hardtack in a cup or pan. Cover
it with water and soak until soft. Fairly fresh hardtack may
require only 15–20 minutes to completely soak through.
But the older the cracker, the longer it will need to soak.

Once the cracker is soft, heat some leftover grease from
fried salt pork in a frying pan. Make sure you use enough
grease to almost cover the hardtack. Fry the hardtack in the
hot grease, turning it once, until both sides are golden
brown. Remove from the pan, salt if desired, and eat.

Hell-Fired Stew

1 square of hardtack
Salt pork grease
Seasoning
Flannel or canvas for pulverizing

This is similar to skillygalee except that the square of hardtack must be pulverized prior to soaking in water. You can pulverize it by wrapping the hardtack in a piece of flannel or canvas, and then pounding it with a rifle butt or a large rock. Shake the resulting crumbs into a frying pan.

Add enough water to thoroughly soak the hardtack crumbs. When they have turned into a soft mass, drain any excess water.

Fry the soaked hardtack in hot salt pork grease until the outside is completely browned. Season and eat.

hardtack that had become tough as nails. While records show that a fair number of men actually liked these concoctions, many more seem to have found them awful. Personally, I find them relatively palatable, although I wouldn't recommend a steady diet of either.

Hardtack Pudding

Always eager to find some way, any way, of adding variety to the standard army marching diet of hardtack, salt pork, and coffee, Billy Yank created hardtack pudding, a tasty off-shoot of hardtack. The recipe below is based on an account mentioned in both William Bircher's *A Drummer Boy's Diary* and in Henry M. Kieffer's *The Recollections of a Drummer Boy*. (No one seems to know who should actually get credit for the recipe.)

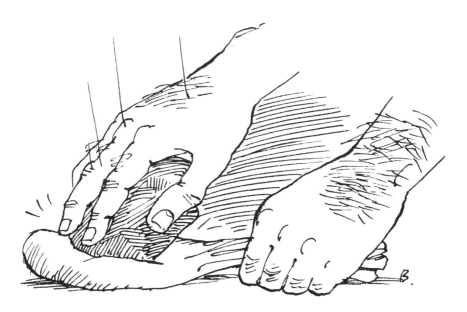

making hardtack pudding

Hardtack Pudding

1 square of hardtack
Heavy cloth bag
Flour
Water
Dried apples
Raisins

Place a single square of hardtack in a bag of heavy cloth such as canvas. On a hard surface, such as a log or rock, beat the cracker into a fine powder with a rifle butt, rock, or large stick. Remove the powder and put it on a plate or in a small mess kettle. Add a handful of flour and stir in enough water to create a stiff dough. Make sure to work the dough until all the dry contents are moistened.

Remove the dough and place on a clean, flat surface such as a mess plate or a kettle lid (hardtack box lids were originally used). Roll flat until it's about $1/8$-inch thick by kneading it from the center outward with the palm of your hand. Cover the dough with chunks of dried apples and a few raisins. Roll the dough, taking care to pinch the open ends closed, and then wrap it in a clean piece of cloth.

Place the wrapped dough in a skillet or mess kettle and add enough water to almost cover it. Boil for about an hour.

Remove dough from the water, open the cloth, scrape out the contents onto a plate or mess tin, and eat.

Cush

Probably one of the best-known Confederate recipes, cush is

mentioned in a number of soldiers' letters and memoirs, testifying

to its popularity. Cush seems to have been the result of the

Confederate army's perennial shortage of cooking utensils, which

necessitated the practice of cooking as much food together as

Cush

1 large chunk cold, cooked beef
Bacon grease
Water
1 piece of cornbread or hardtack

Cut a chunk of cold cooked beef big enough for a meal into small pieces. In a skillet, heat enough bacon grease to cover the frying surface of the pan. Add the beef and fry for a couple of minutes, stirring frequently.

Add enough water to almost cover the beef, then stew the beef in the water about 5 minutes, stirring often, until it is soft.

Crumble a chunk of cornbread or a square of hardtack into the meat and stir well.

Stirring occasionally, cook the cush until the water is absorbed, giving it a hashlike consistency. Your genuine Confederate cush is now ready to eat!

possible. When prepared properly, cush tastes rather good, and many a hungry Confederate soldier looked forward to it as a first-rate supper.

Confederate "Stew"

Mentioned in an unpublished history of the Tenth Mississippi Infantry, Confederate "stew" was concocted out of necessity by soldiers in the Confederate Army of Tennessee during the disastrous retreat from Nashville in the fall of 1864. Despite its western origin, it is undoubtedly representative of the many resourceful, make-it-up-as-you-go cooking efforts of common soldiers in the Confederate armies.

According to the story, the men had beef, flour, potatoes, and a stew pot, but nothing in which to bake their bread. They boiled some beef and potatoes together until nearly done. At that

Confederate Stew
**8-10 oz. beef per person,
cut into bite-sized pieces
2 medium to large potatoes
per person, sliced
Water
Salt and pepper
½ cup flour per person**

Put the beef and the potatoes in a mess kettle and add enough water to cover them. Season with salt and pepper, then boil the mixture for about 45 minutes.

Mix flour with enough water to make the resulting batter flow freely without appearing watery. Add the flapjack batter to the beef and potatoes a spoonful at a time until all the batter is thoroughly mixed in.

As soon as the meat and potatoes are both soft, the stew is ready.

The remains can be left covered in the kettle overnight, allowing them to congeal. Next morning, slice the stew out of the mess kettle and you will have a first class breakfast, as well!

point, someone suggested they use flour to mix up some flapjack batter and add that to the stew. This they did, adding the batter one spoonful at a time until it had all been mixed together. They then ate the lot as stew that night. Next morning, they cut the congealed remains out of the mess kettle, giving each man meat, bread, and potatoes in the same slice.

Yankee Baked Beans

When not actively campaigning, Yankees located in semipermanent encampments were often fortunate enough to receive rations of white beans such as navy beans, one peck (eight quarts) issued per every one hundred rations. Having eaten only hardtack and salt pork for weeks or even months while on campaign (except when he had "liberated" food from the local population), Billy Yank greeted the change in diet enthusiastically. John Billings,

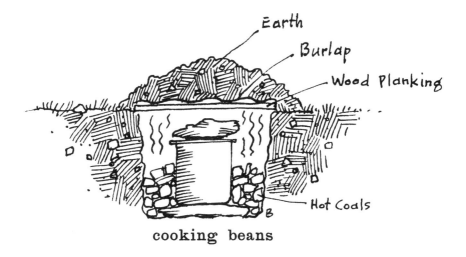

cooking beans

in *Hard Tack and Coffee,* wrote that "the bean ration was an important factor in the sustenance of the Army, and no edible, I think, was so thoroughly appreciated."

The bean ration was often a standard ingredient in soups, mixed with whatever was available at the moment. As you might expect,

Yankee Baked Beans
2 quarts navy or white beans
Water
Raw or cooked salt pork
Salt and pepper
Cayenne pepper

Dig a hole in the ground deep enough to hold a mess kettle of 6-quart capacity or larger and still have an extra foot or so left between the top of the kettle and the top of the hole. If available, place in the bottom of the hole a flat stone big enough for the mess kettle to sit on. Build a large fire in the hole and keep it burning while preparing the beans.

Soak beans in the mess kettle (do not put in the hole yet) for about 3 hours in just enough water to cover them, taking care to add water as the beans absorb it. Add a few small pieces of raw or cooked salt pork for flavor, and salt and pepper to taste. If available, you might also want to add a little cayenne pepper (a very popular seasoning during the war). Place cover on kettle.

(continued)

Yankee Baked Beans (continued)

Shovel the hot coals out of the hole and place the mess kettle in it on top of the flat rock. Cover the kettle with a chunk of wood or another clean, flat rock, and then rake the hot coals back around the sides of the kettle. Carefully place some poles or planks of wood over the hole and cover them with a chunk of burlap sacking or other cloth to exclude dirt from the hole. Shovel enough dirt over the top to completely cover the hole and form a small mound.

Let the beans cook for about 12 hours. Then carefully remove the dirt and planking, remove the kettle, and enjoy some of the best baked beans you'll ever eat!

the New Englanders, in particular, were fond of beans and became known for their practice of baking them.

Parched Corn

During active campaigning, it was a frequent fact of life that the Confederate army would outrun its inadequate commissary system for several days or even weeks at a time. When that occurred, Johnny Reb sometimes found himself scrambling for corn intended for the army's horses and mules. The feed corn was generally dried

Parched Corn

1-2 ears of dried or fresh corn
Bacon fat or salt pork grease
Salt

If already-dried corn isn't available, use fresh corn still in the husk. Pull back the husks and hang the corn up for several days until the kernels are dry enough to be easily removed.

Place the kernels in a skillet with a small amount of bacon fat or salt pork grease. Cover the skillet and place it over a bed of coals. Shaking the skillet frequently, cook the corn until all the kernels have burst, taking care not to let any of them burn. Quickly remove the skillet from the fire and empty the contents into a mess tin or other suitable dish. Salt to taste and eat.

to preserve it for long periods. So, Rebel soldiers were forced to find ways to make the rock-hard kernels chewable and palatable. Most resorted to parching the corn, a process similar to popping popcorn.

Flapjacks

When uncooked flour was issued, flapjacks—a sort of unleavened pancake—were common breakfast and even supper fare on both sides. As previously mentioned, wheat flour shortages in the Confederate army, which appear to have begun by 1862, forced the average Confederate soldier to eat more and more cornbread as the war dragged on. Nevertheless, the frequent capture of Yankee provisions and an occasional flour ration meant that Johnny Reb was nearly as well acquainted with flapjacks as were his Federal opponents.

Both Yankees and Rebels appreciated flapjacks as one of the few tasty meals that even a culinary novice could do a decent job preparing. And flapjacks (also called griddlecakes) were a whole lot simpler to make than bread, not to mention faster. I find the flapjacks quite good, something akin to French crépes in both taste and consistency.

Flapjacks
2-3 spoonfuls of wheat flour
Cold water
A pinch of salt
Salt pork or bacon grease
Honey

Place flour and salt in a cup or mess tin. Slowly stir in cold water until the flour is thoroughly mixed in and the resulting batter is creamy (about the same consistency as regular pancake batter).

Heat just enough salt pork or bacon grease in a skillet to thinly coat the bottom. After the grease has melted, sprinkle a few drops of cold water on the cooking surface: If the water "dances" across the bottom of the skillet for a second or two before evaporating, it's ready. If the water just evaporates, then the skillet is too hot and needs to be moved to a cooler place on the fire; on the other hand, if the water does nothing or takes more than three seconds or so to evaporate, the skillet is too cool.

(continued)

Flapjacks (continued)

Once the skillet heat is correct, pour in the flapjack batter. (Don't make the cakes more than about 3 inches wide or you won't be able to turn them with a knife or fork without breaking them.) Cook the flapjacks until the outer edges of each appear whitish and dry looking. Gently slide a knife or fork under each flapjack (it should lift off the face of the skillet without sticking) and raise it just enough to gently flip it.

Keep cooking the cakes, flipping them until both sides are just starting to brown a little. Remove from the skillet and eat.

If you have a little honey, spread some on top of your flapjacks and treat yourself to a really first-rate meal.

Spices and Seasonings

The official daily ration used by both the Confederate and Federal armies at the beginning of the war included 0.6 ounces of salt, 2.4 ounces of sugar, and 0.32 gills of vinegar. (One gill equals 4 ounces.) In June 1864, the Federal army added 0.04 ounces of pepper in an effort to combat the blandness of army fare.

As was true with other ration items, however, the difference between the amount of seasonings offically provided and what the men actually received was often considerable. When they could afford it, the soldiers sometimes augmented their supply of seasonings and spices by either purchasing them from the sutlers plying their trade just outside camp, or from local civilians. Otherwise, they either improvised or did without.

Cayenne pepper and ginger were popular seasonings during this era. Because they were not a part of army rations, these condiments were usually in even shorter supply than salt or pepper. Some lucky soldiers would receive supplies of these treasured spices in packages sent from home. Others would resort to paying the sutlers' exorbitant prices to satisfy their cravings.

THE SONGS OF THE HUNGRY

 Music played a vital role in soldier life during the war. General Robert E. Lee himself was quoted as saying: "I don't believe we can have an army without music." In an age before radios, cinemas, or the U.S.O., soldiers in the field created their own forms of entertainment, among the most popular of which was singing.

Whether performed a cappella on the march or around the campfire to the accompaniment of a harmonica, fiddle, concertina, or banjo, singing raised the spirits of boys and men a long way from home. It also provided a harmless outlet for commenting on everything from the hardships of army life to the love of a wife or sweetheart back home. Many companies formed official glee clubs that put on "concerts" in camp. Some fortunate regiments even had bands to accompany the glee clubs as they performed repertoires that ran the gamut from rollicking fun to sappy sentimentalism.

Not surprisingly, the theme of a fair number of songs written during the war was food. Some, like "Goober Peas," were simply good fun. A few, like "The Army Bean," were odes to the joy of eating one of the most beloved staples of the army ration. Most,

however, seem to have been good-natured complaints aimed at the
quality, insufficiency, or sheer monotony of army food. Included in
this chapter are some of the favorite songs about army cooking and
army food that soldiers might have heard performed by the
"campfire minstrels" in their units.

"Hard Crackers Come Again No More"

The origin of this song is unclear, although it's often attributed
to the men of the Federal army's First Iowa Regiment. They

reportedly first sang it just prior to the Battle of Wilson's Creek in 1861. Already tired of their steady diet of "hard crackers," these Yankee soldiers borrowed the melody of a popular contemporary song, Stephen Foster's "Hard Times Come Again No More," and turned it into a lament about their monotonous, vermin-infested diet. According to the story, their commanding officer, General Nathaniel Lyon, took pity on their plight and ordered the army's cooks to begin serving cornmeal mush. Not long afterwards, the steady diet of army mush prompted a new chorus to the song: "Hard crackers come again once more." There just wasn't any pleasing some people!

"Goober Peas"

This Confederate camp song was one of the most popular of the war. "Goobers" were simply peanuts, which, as the Yankee blockade of Southern ports wore on, became an increasingly important part of the Rebel soldier's diet. Georgia soldiers in particular were associated with eating peanuts and were commonly referred to as "goober grabbers." No one knows who first invented this light-hearted tune. When it first appeared in print after the war in 1866, credit was given to "P. Nutt, Esq." and "A. Pindar."

"The Army Bean"

As noted earlier, Federal soldiers in camp often enjoyed a ration of beans. After weeks or even months of living on hardtack and salt pork, beans were a welcome change in diet. "The Army Bean," sung to the tune of "The Sweet Bye and Bye," celebrates this simple pleasure.

As with many songs that got their start around a wartime campfire, no one knows who wrote the lyrics to "The Army Bean." According to John Billings, this song also did not appear in print until after the "Late Unpleasantness" was over.

"Short Rations"

The Confederate armies operating in the western part of the country suffered far greater privations than their counterparts in the East. Unlike the relatively compact eastern theater (centered primarily around northern and eastern Virginia), the western theater covered thousands of square miles across several states. To make matters worse, large western rivers like the Mississippi and the Tennessee ran north-south instead of east-west like the rivers in Virginia, making them at once barriers to the movement of men and supplies for the Confederates and watery highways into the heart of the Confederacy for the Yankees.

"Short Rations," dedicated to the "Corn-Fed Army of Tennessee," tells the tale of hunger and suffering faced by the Confederate soldier in the West and blames everyone from speculators to politicians to army staff officers for the woes of the common private. Although the author of the lyrics is anonymous, John Alcee Augustin, a soldier in the Confederate Army of Tennessee, wrote the music.

"A Life on the Vicksburg Bluff"

The Confederate Army of Vicksburg and the inhabitants of Vicksburg, Mississippi, endured a horrific siege that began with the repulse of the second Federal assault on the Vicksburg defenses on May 22, 1863, and lasted forty-three days. Finally, on July 4, 1863, with the army and civilians alike reduced to eating mule meat and rats, General John C. Pemberton, commander of the Confederate garrison, surrendered his army to Ulysses S. Grant, the Federal commander. Fully half of the surrendered Confederate soldiers were too weak or too sick to fight.

"A Life on the Vicksburg Bluff," written by A. Dalsheimer, a soldier in the Third Louisiana Infantry during the siege, tells of both the hunger and the artillery bombardment. Henry Russell, an Englishman who lived in the U.S. from 1833 to 1841, wrote the music in 1838, and it was popular both before and during the war. "Pea-bread," mentioned in the song, was coarse, dark bread made by mixing ground field peas with either cornmeal or wheat flour. It became an increasingly common replacement for regular bread in the Confederate army as reliable sources of food became scarce. "Old Logan's" beef may refer to Federal Major General John A. Logan, commander of the Third Division of Major General James B. McPherson's Seventeenth Corps (part of the Federal force besieging Vicksburg), although the reference is not clear.

Hard Crackers Come Again No More

Goober Peas

Reprinted with permission from *Songs of the Civil War,*
Irwin Sibler, Dover Publications, Inc.

2. When a horseman passes, the soldiers have a rule,
   To cry out at their loudest, "Mister, here's your mule!"
   But another pleasure enchantinger than these,
   Is wearing out your grinders, eating goober peas! (Chorus)

3. Just before the battle the Gen'ral hears a row,
   He says, "The Yanks are coming, I hear their rifles now."
   He turns around in wonder, and what do you think he sees?
   The Georgia Militia—eating goober peas! (Chorus)

4. I think my song has lasted almost long enough,
   The subject's interesting, but rhymes are mighty rough,
   I wish this war was over, when free from rags and fleas,
   We'd kiss our wives and sweethearts and gobble goober peas! (Chorus)

The Army Bean

fore; The ar - my bean, nice and clean, We'll___ stick to our beans ev - er - more. more.

2.
Now the bean in its primitive state
Is a plant we have all often met;
And when cooked in the old army style
It has charms we can never forget.

Chorus: 'Tis the bean, etc.

3.
The German is fond of sauerkraut,
The potato is loved by the Mick,
But the soldiers have long since found out
That through life to our beans we should stick.

Chorus: 'Tis the bean, etc.

Short Rations

Fair la – dies and maids___ of all a – ges, Lit – tle girls___ and ca – dets___ how – e'er youth – ful, Home guards, quar – ter – mas – ters and sa – ges, Who___ write for the news – pa – pers so

Short Rations (continued)

Chorus

For we sol - diers have seen some-thing rough - er, Than a storm,__ a re-treat,__ or a fight, And the bod - y may toil__ on and suf - fer, With a smile, so the heart is all right!

2.

Our bugles had roused up the camp,
  The heavens look'd dismal and dirty,
And the earth look'd unpleasant and damp,
  As a beau on the wrong side of thirty.
We were taking these troubles with quiet,
  When we heard from the mouths of some rash ones,
That the army was all put on diet,
  And the Board had diminished our rations.

Chorus: For we soldiers, etc.

3.

Reduce our rations at all?
  It was difficult, yet it was done,
We had one meal a day, it was small,
  Are we now, oh! ye gods! to have none?
Oh! ye gentlemen issuing rations,
  Give at least half her own to the State,
Put a curb on your maddening passions,
  And commissaries commisserate!

Chorus: For we soldiers, etc.

4.

Erewhiles we had chickens and roasters,
  For the fowls and pigs were ferocious,
We would sent them to short Pater Nosters,
  And the deed was not stamped as atrocious;
But since men have been shot for the same,
  We parch corn, it is healthier, but tougher —
The chickens and pigs have got tame,
  But the horses and mules have to suffer.

Chorus: For we soldiers, etc.

5.

But the "Corn-fed" is proof to all evils,
  Has a joke for all hardships and troubles,
In honor and glory he revels,
  Other fancies he looks on as bubbles!
He is bound to be free, and he knows it,
  Then what cares he for toil and privation!
He is brave, and in battle he shows it,
  And will conquer in spite of starvation.

Chorus: For we soldiers, etc.

A Life on the Vicksburg Bluff

1. A life on the Vicks - burg bluff, _____ A _____ home in the trench - es deep, _____ Where we dodge "Yank" shells e - nough, _____ And our old "pea-bread" won't keep. _____ On "old Lo - gan's" beef I pine, _____ For there's fat on his bones no

A Life on the Vicksburg Bluff (continued)

bread,_____ pea - bread_____ Our old pea-bread won't keep,_____ Pea -

bread,_____ pea - bread,_____ Our old pea-bread won't keep._____ keep._____

2.

Old Grant is starving us out,
  Our grub is fast wasting away,
Pemb' don't know what he's about,
  And he hasn't for many a day,
So we'll bury "old Logan" tonight,
  From tough beef we'll be set free;
We'll put him far out of sight,
  No more of his meat for me.
A life on the Vicksburg bluff, etc.

3.

Texas steers are no longer in view,
  Mule steaks are now "done up brown,"
While peabread, mule roast and mule stew,
  Are our fare in Vicksburg town;
And the song of our hearts shall be,
  While the Yanks and their gunboats rave;
A life in a bomb-proof for me,
  And a tear on "old Logan's" grave.
A life on the Vicksburg bluff, etc.

PASSING TIME AWAY

 Singing and making music were not the only ways the soldiers kept their minds off empty stomachs, bad food, and the dangers of war. Between the mind-numbing routine of drill and chores when in camp, and the sheer terror and adrenaline rush of combat, the men on both sides found many other ways to occupy their time.

Letter Writing

Without a doubt, exchanging letters with loved ones and friends back home was the soldier's most cherished pastime. Lucius Barber, who served as a sergeant in the Fifteenth Illinois Volunteer Infantry, recalled in later years that "it was the one great joy of camp life to receive kind and encouraging words from our friends." The company first sergeant's cry of "Mail call!" was sure to create a stampede. Almost instantly, he would find himself surrounded by a jostling sea of expectant faces, each waiting to find out if he, too, would be the lucky recipient of long-awaited news from family and friends in the outside world.

Soldiers wrote wherever and whenever they could. The back of a knapsack, a drumhead, a tin plate, the lid of a hardtack box balanced on one's knees, or one's knees themselves—any surface served as a makeshift writing desk. At times, a soldier's letter writing might be interrupted by the need to put down his pen and take up arms. Upon concluding his participation in the hostilities, he would again take up his pen and, after a brief apology or explanation to the letter's recipient, continue writing.

Early in the war, paper, pens, and ink were plentiful on both sides of the Mason-Dixon Line. Indeed, camp sutlers and the Christian Commission made sure the northern boys were well supplied throughout the war with writing utensils, although the soldiers had to occasionally resort to writing in pencil while actively campaigning due to ink shortages. Yankee letter writers also had plenty of writing paper and envelopes, some even printed with fancy patriotic designs.

> **Because of paper shortages, Rebels resorted to erasing letters they received written in pencil and then writing their own letters over the smudged remains.**

Confederate soldiers, on the other hand, began experiencing shortages of paper, ink, and pens after only a few months of war. But Johnny Reb was nothing if not resourceful. He learned to make ink from pokeberry juice or oak galls, and a serviceable pen from goose quill, cornstalk, or well-whittled sticks. Because of paper shortages, letter-writing Rebels even resorted to erasing letters they received written in pencil and then writing their own letters over the smudged remains. Another popular method of paper conservation was writing one's letter between the lines of a letter received from home.

The styles of the letters varied as much as the education and background of the men writing them. Some were flowing and eloquent, while others were crude and almost childish in their simplicity. The majority fell somewhere in between. Regardless of the writer's skill, however, the letters quickly revealed their writers' abiding love for those back home, as well as their feelings of homesickness and their need to stay in touch with the outside world.

Just as letters from home lifted the soldier's spirits and gave him vital information about the world he left behind, the letters he wrote from the front provided his family and friends with cherished news about his health and whereabouts. In addition, they were frequently filled with stories of camp life and descriptions of battles. Just as important, they often contained the latest news about other family members and mutual friends also serving in the army.

Writing letters was one thing. Getting them to their intended destination was quite another. Early in the war, Federal soldiers were required to use postage stamps. More than one Yankee opened his pocket after a hard day's march to find that his sweat had soaked through his shirt and caused his wad of stamps to congeal into a useless blob of paper. Luckily, the Postmaster General eventually issued an order allowing soldiers to simply write "Soldier's Letter" on the envelope in lieu of affixing a stamp, thereby doing away with the need for stamps.

Southern soldiers, on the other hand, confronted even greater obstacles. Many a Reb could ill afford stamps. Under Confederate postal regulations, soldiers were allowed to send letters postage-due. But many men hesitated to take advantage of this, since the folks back home were often just as poor as the soldiers were. So, likely as not, Johnny Reb entrusted delivery of his letters to men going home on furlough, visitors, clergy, servants—basically anyone who didn't run away fast enough.

Pranks, Practical Jokes, and General Mischief

Except for corresponding with friends and family back home, nothing provided Johnny Reb or Billy Yank with as much entertainment and relief from the hardships of army life as playing practical jokes. The boys also created a variety of funny expressions and spent a lot of off-duty time just horsing around.

Perhaps no expression on either side was more famous than "Here's your mule," the Confederate soldiers' all-purpose expression for everything under the sun. No one knows how it started. However, it's often attributed to soldiers under the command of the dashing Confederate cavalryman John Hunt Morgan. Wherever Morgan's men camped during their second Kentucky raid, local mules had a bad habit of disappearing. One farmer, infuriated by the loss of his finest mule, marched into Morgan's camp demanding that his mule be immediately returned. From somewhere in the camp, a voice yelled out, "Hey, Mister— here's your mule!" As the unsuspecting farmer stomped off in the direction of the voice, yet another soldier, in a completely different part of the camp, took up the cry. Pretty soon, the entire camp was

Except for corresponding with friends and family back home, nothing provided as much entertainment and relief from the hardships of army life as playing practical jokes.

in a frenzy, with soldiers everywhere shouting, "Here's your mule!" until the poor farmer, completely exasperated, beat a hasty retreat.

Visiting civilians were frequently the targets of jokes and pranks, especially if they wore expensive or unusual clothing. One Yankee, Charles Wills, recorded such an incident near Atlanta in his diary: One of his fellow soldiers, upon seeing a man in civilian clothes riding a bony, down-trodden old horse through their encampment, yelled out a loud "caw-caw-caw." Upon hearing him, the rest of the men in camp immediately responded in return, until it sounded as if "10,000 crows were holding a jubilee."

New recruits were a favorite target; both Yanks and Rebs delighted in teasing, terrifying, and harassing the nervous rookie soldiers until they were deemed acceptable as members of the unit.

Fellow soldiers were also prime targets for some good-natured fun. Bromfield Ridley, a first lieutenant on Confederate Major General A. P. Stewart's staff, recorded how a Rebel passing a friend marching in the other direction called out, "How are you,

Jim?" This cued the rest of his comrades to join in until Jim was overwhelmed by the greetings of an entire division. A soldier with a new hat would invariably hear comments such as: "Take that camp kettle home! Aren't you ashamed to steal some poor soldier's camp kettle?" or "Come out of that hat! I see your legs!"

When it came to practical jokes, new recruits were a favorite target. Both Yanks and Rebs delighted in teasing, terrifying, and harassing the nervous rookie soldiers until they were deemed acceptable as members of the unit. One favorite prank involved assigning a new man to night guard duty. The assignment was accompanied by stern warnings from the old veterans about the potential dangers, and the need for vigilance and the courage to die at a moment's notice for one's country and comrades. Unknown to the now-terrified recruit, he was manning his post with a rifle that his messmates had earlier unloaded. Pie-eyed with fear, the greenhorn would stand peering into the forbidding darkness for any signs of lurking danger. After sufficient time had passed, his comrades would come crunching and crackling through the underbrush in front of the guard post. Doing their level best to stifle their giggles, they would then charge the poor wretch's position as he vainly attempted to get off a warning shot.

Not nearly as terrifying for a new recruit, but every bit as humiliating, was the practice of larking, a game many a modern-day Boy Scout would recognize. Sam Watkins, in his entertaining memoir *Co. Aytch: A Sideshow of the Big Show,* described a larking that occurred in the Confederate First Tennessee Infantry Regiment:

> *At this place, we took Walter Hood out "a larking." The way to go "a larking" is this: Get an empty meal bag and about a dozen men and go to some dark forest or open field on some cold, dark, frosty or rainy night, about five miles from camp. Get someone who does not understand the game to hold the bag in as stooping and cramped a position as possible, keep perfectly still and quiet, and when he has got in the right fix, the others to go off and drive in the larks. As soon as they get out of sight, they break in a run and go back to camp, and go to sleep, leaving the poor fellow all the time holding the bag.*

Snowball Fights

During winter weather, the incessant drilling and fatigue duty that marked the rest of the year relaxed significantly. This left large numbers of healthy, active young men with precious little to do to keep themselves from going stir-crazy. While activities such as sledding and making snowmen, or snow effigies, as they were called at the time, were sometimes popular, by far the most entertaining winter sport was snowball fighting.

What began as spur-of-the-moment snowball fights between two or three men often mushroomed into huge contests involving hundreds, even thousands of men. Companies—even entire regiments or divisions—would take to the field with drums and bugles sounding, and sword-waiving officers directing their troops in pitched battles that could last for hours. Bell Wiley, in his book *The Life of Billy Yank,* quoted a Federal soldier, George T. Stevens, underscoring the ferocity of many snowball fights with this eyewitness account of a battle between the Twenty-sixth New Jersey Regiment and an unnamed Vermont regiment:

> *Both regiments formed a line of battle, each officered by its line and field officers, the latter mounted. At the signal the battle commenced; charges and counter-charges were made, prisoners were taken on either side, and the air was filled with white missiles and stentorian cheers went up as one or other party gained an advantage. At length, victory rested with the Vermonters, and the Jersey boys surrendered the field defeated.*

However, no recorded snowball fight on either side ever rivaled the fame of the Great Dalton Snowball Fight. On March 22, 1864, a late snow hit the Confederate Army of Tennessee while it was encamped near Dalton, Georgia. The battle, which first began as a series of skirmishes, quickly grew into full-scale combat, pitting the Tenth and Forty-fourth Mississippi Infantry Regiments against the Forty-first Mississippi Infantry Regiment, reinforced by the Seventh and Ninth Mississippi Infantry Regiments. The crowning event of the day, however, was the battle between the divisions of Benjamin Cheatham and William Walker, in which an estimated five to six thousand men hurled snowballs at each other for three hours.

Although the soldiers always considered them great fun, snowball fights were far from being genteel affairs: Snowballs filled with rocks were not uncommon, and many letters and diaries attest to the presence of broken bones, knocked-out teeth, black eyes, and bloody noses among the casualties of the snowball wars. War, even one fought with handfuls of frozen slush, is indeed hell.

Games and Gambling

Both Johnny Reb and Billy Yank also enjoyed playing various types of games in their off-duty hours. Checkers, or draughts, as it was often known, was a popular board game. Chess, while certainly not unheard of, was seen less frequently. Friendly games of cards were also common. These diversions paled, however, in comparison to the gambling that ran rampant through both armies.

Sometimes vilified or banned by the officers, other times tolerated or even encouraged, gambling was for many their greatest pastime. The soldiers gambled on virtually anything, from boxing matches to cockfights to footraces. When in camp, a gambling

soldier might spend up to six hours a day playing games of chance, and many a warrior went flat broke before the sun set on payday.

One of the most common ways the boys parted with their money was over the dice game of chuck-a-luck, also known as sweat, in which one would roll three dice on a board or a piece of cloth that had been divided into numbered squares. While the game was entertaining, those who lost their wagers far outnumbered the few who won big: "… I always noticed that chuck won," wrote Sam Watkins of the Confederate First Tennessee Infantry, "and luck always lost."

Other popular gambling games included craps and even roulette. However, card games such as poker, faro, euchre, and even cribbage, were by far the most popular games with the Civil War gamblers. Reportedly, some men became so absorbed in their high-stakes card games that they would even risk their lives. One Yankee artilleryman, Alfred S. Roe, wrote of an occasion when a group of poker players persisted in finishing their hand, despite being under direct fire from Rebel artillery. After finishing the hand, they then moved behind a large tree and continued playing!

Fraternizing and Trading
with the Enemy

The Civil War created a tangled web of conflicting emotions

and sentiments on both sides. Decades of mistrust and disagreement

over some of the most important economic, political, and social

issues of the day had turned families and

friends into bitter enemies. Northerners

and Southerners, turned enemies, had

been fellow citizens of a country whose

independence had been secured less than

a century before by their grandfathers

Perhaps it stands to reason that the warriors on both sides developed a grudging respect and admiration for each other.

and great-grandfathers, who had fought

together for a common cause. U.S.–Mexican War veterans who had

gone on to serve in the Union and Confederate armies were firing

on the very men with whom they had just previously fought side by

side. Others had visited or even lived in the region that was now the

country of their enemy.

Of course, just as the war itself has sometimes been

romanticized, incidents of fraternization and soldierly camaraderie may have been exaggerated. It is true, though, that Johnny Reb and Billy Yank occasionally did find themselves face-to-face off the field of battle. In these instances, the war was put aside for a few moments.

Wherever the opposing lines were within shouting distance, pickets from each side were likely to strike up a conversation.

Sometimes, these conversations consisted of little more than the bantering of insults back and forth. Other times, especially when the front-line positions were static and there was little threat of combat, mutual suspicion and caution gradually gave way to trust and even friendship of a sort.

Bruce Catton, in his book *Reflections on the Civil War,* reports an instance where pickets facing each other across the Rappahannock River in Virginia became acquainted and began trading with each other. By mutual agreement, the Yankee boys loaded toy boats they had constructed from wooden planks with bags of coffee and set them to sail across the river and into the eager hands of the caffeine-deprived Confederates on the other side. The Rebels returned the boats loaded with good Virginia tobacco, to the delight of the boatbuilders.

Before long, trading for mutual benefit gave way to feelings of genuine friendship. One night, the Rebel boys invited their Yankee friends to come across the river and join them at a dance being held a short ways beyond the river. Sure enough, a half dozen unarmed Yankees made their way across the river and had a hooting good time at the dance—until a very agitated Confederate officer found them out and attempted to have them arrested as prisoners of war. Their hosts begged the officer not to do this, lest he besmirch their honor, since they had given their word to the Yankees that they would be safe. At last, the officer relented, and, after pinning his men's ears back with a so-help-me-I'll-shoot-you-next-time lecture on the evils of fraternizing with the enemy, allowed the Yankee boys to cross back over the river unharmed.

Northerner and Southerner, Yankee and Rebel, Americans all— right to the bitter end.

BIBLIOGRAPHY

Barber, Lucius W. *Army Memoirs*. Chicago: The J. M. W. Jones Stationery and Printing Company, 1894; reprint edition, Alexandria, VA: Time-Life Books, 1984.

Billings, John D. *Hard Tack and Coffee*. Boston: George M. Smith and Company, 1887; reprint edition, Alexandria, VA: Time-Life Books, 1982.

Catton, Bruce. *Bruce Catton's Civil War*. Vol. I: *Mr. Lincoln's Army*. New York: Fairfax Press, 1984.

_____. *Reflections on the Civil War*. Edited by John Leekley. New York: Doubleday and Company, 1981.

Daniel, Larry J. *Soldiering in the Army of Tennessee*. Chapel Hill, NC: The University of North Carolina Press, 1991.

Davis, Charles E. "Three Years in the Army." In *The Blue and the Gray,* p. 278. Edited by Henry Steele Commager. New York: Fairfax Press, 1982.

Davis, William C. *The Civil War Cookbook*. Philadelphia: Courage Books, 1993.

Fletcher, William A. *Rebel Private: Front and Rear*. Beaumont, Texas: Press of the Greer print, 1908; reprint edition, New York: Meridian, 1997.

Kory, Elizabeth Stroud. *1862 Manual for Army Cooking*. Norristown, PA: Norristown Press, 1993.

McCarthy, Carlton. *Detailed Minutiae of Soldier Life in the Army of Northern Virginia.* Richmond: Carlton McCarthy and Company, 1882; reprint edition, Lincoln, Nebraska: University of Nebraska Press, 1993.

Mitchell, Patricia B. *Confederate Camp Cooking.* Chatham, VA: By the Author. Sims-Mitchell House Bed and Breakfast, 1991.

Ridley, Bromfield. "Battles and Sketches of the Army of Tennessee." In *The Blue and the Gray,* p. 440. Edited by Henry Steele Commager. New York: Fairfax Press, 1982.

Silber, Irwin, ed. *Songs of the Civil War.* New York: Dover Publications, Inc., 1995.

Time-Life Books, Inc., gen. ed. *The Civil War.* 27 vols. Alexandria, VA: Time-Life Books, 1983–1987. Vol. 3: *Tenting Tonight,* by James I. Robertson, Jr.

United States War Department. *War of the Rebellion. A Compilation of the Official Records of the Union and Confederate Armies.* 128 vols. Washington, DC: 1881–1902.

Watkins, Sam R. *Co. Aytch: A Sideshow of the Big Show.* Nashville, TN: Cumberland Presbyterian Publishing House, 1882; reprint ed., Wilmington, NC: Broadfoot Publishing Company, 1990.

Wiley, Bell Irvin. *The Life of Billy Yank: The Common Soldier of the Union.* Baton Rouge: Louisiana State University Press, 1952; reprint ed., Baton Rouge: Louisiana State University Press, 1978.

_____. *The Life of Johnny Reb: The Common Soldier of the Confederacy.* Baton Rouge: Louisiana State University Press, 1943; reprint ed., Baton Rouge: Louisiana State University Press, 1978.

ACKNOWLEDGMENT

I am greatly indebted to the generous assistance of Mr. Bobby Horton, who from his own extensive collection of Civil War music graciously provided me with the music and lyrics to several of the songs presented in this book. You are, sir, a true southern gentleman. This book would have been much the poorer without your kindness.

GARRY FISHER is an avid reader and collector of works on the Civil War. *Rebel Cornbread and Yankee Coffee*, which is his first book, is the result of extensive research conducted during the last ten years. Fisher is a lifelong Civil War enthusiast, a member of the Sons of Confederate Veterans, and a former member of the Los Angeles Civil War Round Table. He, his wife, and their two children live in Winston-Salem, North Carolina.

HARRY BLAIR is an illustrator and history buff who lives in Greensboro, North Carolina.